⊕ WORLD BOOK'S

CELEBRATIONS AND RITUALS AROUND THE WORLD

World Book, Inc.
a Scott Fetzer Company
Chicago

This edition published in the United States of America by World Book, Inc., Chicago. WORLD BOOK and the GLOBE DEVICE are registered trademarks or trademarks of World Book, Inc.

World Book, Inc.
233 North Michigan Avenue
Chicago, IL 60601 U.S.A.

For information about other World Book publications, visit our Web site http://www.worldbook.com, or call 1-800-WORLDBK (967-5325).
For information about sales to schools and libraries, call: 1-800-975-3250 (United States); 1-800-837-5365 (Canada).

In the same series:
Birth and Growing Up Celebrations
Harvest Celebrations
New Year's Celebrations
Spring Celebrations

Copyright © 2003, McRae Books Srl

Via dei Rustici, 5—Florence, Italy.
info@mcraebooks.com

Library of Congress Cataloging-in-Publication Data
National celebrations.
    p. cm. —(World Book's celebrations and rituals around the world)
    Includes index.
    Summary: Describes how special events or people in the history of a nation are celebrated in different countries, by different cultures, and with different foods around the world. Includes recipes and activities.
    ISBN: 0-7166-5009-6
    1. Holidays—Cross-cultural studies—Juvenile literature.
2. Festivals—Cross-cultural studies—Juvenile literature. [1. Holidays.
2. Festivals. 3. Nationalism] I. World Book, Inc. II. Series.
GT3933 .N37 2002
394.26--dc21   2002027046

Printed and bound in Hong Kong by C&C Offset

1 2 3 4 5 6 7 8 9 10 09 08 07 06 05 04 03 02

McRae Books:
Publishers: Anne McRae and Marco Nardi
Series Editor: Loredana Agosta
Graphic Design: Marco Nardi
Layout: Sebastiano Ranchetti
Picture Research: Loredana Agosta, Leah Coffey
Cutouts: Filippo delle Monache, Alman Graphic Design
Text: Matilde Bardi p. 7; Catherine Chambers pp. 38–41; Anita Ganeri pp. 10–17; Neil Morris pp. 8–9, 22–37, 42–43; Cath Senker pp. 18–21

Illustrations: Inklink Firenze, Studio Stalio (Alessandro Cantucci, Fabiano Fabbrucci, Andrea Morandi, Ivan Stalio), MM Illustrazione (Manuela Cappon and Valeria Grimaldi) Luisa Della Porta, Paola Ravaglia, Paula Holguín, Antonella Pastorelli

Color Separations: Litocolor, Florence (Italy)

World Book:
Editorial: Maureen Liebenson, Sharon Nowakowski
Research: Paul Kobasa, Cheryl Graham, Karen McCormack
Text Processing: Curley Hunter, Gwendolyn Johnson
Proofreading: Anne Dillon

Acknowledgements
The Publishers would like to thank the following photographers and picture libraries for the photos used in this book.
t=top; tl=top left; tc=top center; tr=top right; c=center; cl=center left; cr=center right; b= bottom; bl=bottom left; bc=bottom center; br=bottom right
Lonely Planet Images: Richard l'Anson 12bl; Marco Lanza: 21br, 33tr, 35br, 43bl; The Image Works: 3b, 6cl, 6br, 8br, 9tr, 11b, 13tr, 13b, 15c, 16b, 17tr, 17 bl, 20br, 21tr, 23tr, 25cl, 25b, 28cl, 29c, 29br, 33tl, 33b, 35tr, 36cl, 36b, 39tr, 40bl, 41cr, 41cl, 42b

WORLD BOOK'S
CELEBRATIONS AND RITUALS AROUND THE WORLD

NATIONAL
CELEBRATIONS

Table of Contents

National Celebrations

Introduction

A British soldier was also known as a "redcoat" during the Revolutionary War in America. The war led to American independence and the formation of the United States of America.

This ivory carving from Benin shows a Portuguese soldier taking slaves for trade. European plantations in the Americas created a demand for African slaves in the 1500's. Millions of Africans were taken from their native countries.

National holidays celebrate special events or people that represent freedom, sacrifice, and courage in the history of a nation. Festivities often include speeches by heads of state or government, commemorative ceremonies, firework displays, parades, sporting events, and family get-togethers. In the United States, July 4, also called Independence Day, commemorates the day in 1776 when the original 13 colonies declared their independence from Great Britain by adopting the Declaration of Independence. The whole country celebrates this holiday. But there are other groups within the United States that celebrate their own special people or events. In recent years, growing numbers of African Americans have begun celebrating Juneteenth in memory of the day in June 1865 when the slaves of Texas learned they were free. People in many other countries hold national holidays, too. People in Africa, Asia, and South America remember the efforts needed to win their independence from their European rulers. In France, Bastille Day, held on July 14, celebrates the day when ordinary people stormed a hated prison where political prisoners were kept.

NATIONAL HOLIDAYS THROUGH THE YEAR

JANUARY
6 Maroon festival, Jamaica
26 Australia Day

FEBRUARY
6 Waitangi Day, New Zealand

MARCH
1 Yap Day, Micronesia; Samil Movement festival, Korea
25 Greek Independence Day

APRIL
25 Anzac Day; Italian Liberation Day
27 Freedom Day, South Africa

MAY
3 Constitution Memorial Day, Japan

JUNE
12 Philippine Independence Day

JULY
4 U.S. Independence Day
14 Bastille Day, France

AUGUST
15 Indian Independence Day; Pakistani Independence Day
17 Indonesian Independence Day
31 Merdeka Day, Malaysia

SEPTEMBER
7 Brazilian Independence Day
16 Mexican Independence Day

OCTOBER
3 Day of German Unity

NOVEMBER
5 Guy Fawkes Day

DECEMBER
10 Constitution Day, Thailand

India's mighty elephant, guided by Mohandas Gandhi, is shown standing up to the British lion. India achieved independence in 1947 with Mohandas Gandhi as the leader of the nationalist movement. The people called Gandhi the Mahatma, "Great Soul."

Kwame Nkrumah, who is depicted on the back of this woman's dress, became Ghana's first leader after independence. Ghana, formerly known as the Gold Coast, gained its independence from Britain in 1957.

UNITED NATIONS #68

1¢

NACIONES UNIDAS · NATIONS UNIES

ОБЪЕДИНЕННЫЕ НАЦИИ

The founding of the United Nations in 1945 is commemorated on this postage stamp.

A Yanomami woman prepares cassava flour. The Yanomami people are native to the Amazonian rain forests of southern Venezuela and northern Brazil.

Ancient Cultures

The Dalai Lama is the spiritual head of Tibetan Buddhism. In 1959, he was forced into exile in India after an unsuccessful uprising against Chinese forces occupying Tibet. The Dalai Lama won the Nobel Peace Prize in 1989.

Preserving Traditions

Throughout history, indigenous peoples (people who are native to a country or region) all over the world have been threatened and often conquered by more powerful newcomers from other cultures. Often, conquered people lost their traditional ways of life and customs. In recent times, however, many indigenous peoples have won new respect for their native culture, as well as rights to their ancestral lands. Now, new festivals and holidays commemorate regained peace and freedom.

A Pueblo chief maintains a centuries-old tradition of authority among his people, who live mainly in the U.S. states of New Mexico and Arizona.

Indigenous People's Day

August 9 has been declared the International Day of the World's Indigenous People by the United Nations. First celebrated in 1995, this holiday reminds people of the indigenous societies that exist all over the world. The United Nations is particularly concerned about the human rights, economic development, education, and health of native peoples, as well as the environment in which they live. Every year, the United Nations invites governments, embassies, universities, and other organizations to celebrate this special day.

The flag of the United Nations shows a map of the world surrounded by olive branches, which are symbolic of peace.

This Ainu woman wears traditional blue tattooing around her mouth. She is a native of the Japanese island of Hokkaido.

Political Exile

Throughout history and around the world, oppressive governments have forced people to give up their beliefs, traditional customs, and even their language. Many have suffered the destruction of their cultural heritage, including books, paintings, monuments, and places of worship. In 2001, for example, in Afghanistan, statues of Buddha were destroyed by an extreme Islamic regime. Some groups have fled or been forced to leave their native land and to seek asylum elsewhere. Some exiles are political or religious leaders, while others are ordinary people wishing to live peaceful lives.

Celebrating Freedom

Many festivals celebrate peace and freedom from oppression. Each year on January 6, the Maroons of Jamaica celebrate the date in 1738 when they signed a peace treaty with the British who ruled Jamaica. The British had captured the Caribbean island of Jamaica from Spain 83 years earlier, but many of the Spaniards' black slaves had escaped into the mountains. There they formed bands called Maroons, who harassed the British inhabitants.

Drums beat out the rhythm at a Jamaican Maroon festival.

Keeping Traditional Cultures Alive

The Pacific island of Yap is one of the Caroline Islands, which form part of the Federated States of Micronesia. The Carolines were formally claimed by Spain in 1885. In 1899, they were sold to Germany. Micronesia finally gained its independence, in free association with the United States, in 1986. Every March 1, Yap Day, the Yapese celebrate their unique culture, performing traditional dances, games, and tests of skill such as spear-throwing. Local farmers show off their best produce, including coconuts, bananas, taros (large, starchy underground stems), yams, and sweet potatoes.

A traditional dance of the conquest is performed by the Quiché people of Guatemala in remembrance of their Mayan descent. The dance tells the story of how their land was taken by Spanish conquerors in the 1500's.

Yapese dancers wear traditional grass skirts. Each dance tells a different story.

JAPAN AND KOREA

Japan treasures its ancient culture and traditions. Between the 1600's and the 1800's, the country remained isolated from the outside world and closed to foreigners. Today, Japan ranks as one of the world's leading industrial and technological powers. Despite their country's transformation, however, the Japanese remain proud of their traditional customs.

In 1948, the country of Korea was divided in two—Communist North Korea and democratic South Korea. The flag of South Korea was adopted in 1950. The yin-yang symbol, above, appears on the flag and stands for the opposing but harmonious forces of nature.

The Japanese war cabinet *plans the invasion of Korea.*

The Far East

Becoming a Major Power

In the late 1800's, Japan began to expand its territories. By developing along European lines, it became a major colonial power. By the early 1900's, it gained control of Korea and part of Manchuria on the Asian mainland. In 1904 and 1905, Japan fought a war with Russia and defeated them, gaining control of a Russian port and naval base in Manchuria. In World War I (1914-1918), Japan ousted the Germans from China and occupied German-held Pacific islands. During World War II (1939-1945), Japan continued to expand its control of Southeast Asia. On December 7, 1941, the Japanese attacked Pearl Harbor, a United States naval base in Hawaii. This event proved to be a turning point in the war, bringing the United States into the conflict and marking the eventual end of Japanese expansion.

A Japanese flag is displayed by U.S. soldiers who captured it during World War II.

Great celebrations filled Japanese streets when Japan defeated Russia *in the Russo-Japanese War of 1904–1905.*

THE FAR EAST

The Far East is the easternmost part of Asia. Asia extends from Africa and Europe in the west to the Pacific Ocean in the east. The northernmost part of the continent is in the Arctic. In the south, Asia ends in the tropics near the equator. Traditionally, the term Far East has referred to China, Japan, North Korea, South Korea, Taiwan, and eastern Siberia in Russia. Southeast Asia includes Borneo, Brunei, Cambodia, East Timor, Indonesia, Laos, Malaysia, Myanmar, the Philippines, Singapore, Thailand, and Vietnam.

The New Constitution

Japan finally agreed to end the war on August 14, 1945, after the United States dropped atomic bombs on two Japanese cities. After its defeat, Japan was occupied by Allied troops until they officially left in 1952. Under U.S. authority, the Japanese drew up a new Constitution, which went into effect on May 3, 1947. The Constitution banned Japan from waging war or keeping an army and guaranteed human rights. The emperor could no longer claim to be a god, and control of the country was to pass to the Japanese people. Each year, the Japanese celebrate May 3 as a national holiday called Constitution Memorial Day.

The Samil Movement in *Korea is commemorated in this postage stamp.*

Children celebrate during a Samil Movement festival.

Samil Movement

In 1910, Japan conquered Korea. Life became hard for the Korean people, and they began to call for freedom from Japanese rule. On March 1, 1919, a group of Korean cultural and religious leaders signed a declaration of independence, which was read to a huge crowd in Seoul, the capital city. This triggered a nationwide independence movement known as the Samil Movement. Thousands of Koreans were killed, wounded, or arrested in the demonstrations that followed. On March 1 each year, Koreans celebrate a national holiday to honor the freedom fighters.

Koreans march and wave banners during a festival in honor of the Samil Movement.

Southeast Asia

Southeast Asia is made up of a mainland peninsula and thousands of islands. It includes 12 countries—Borneo, Brunei, Cambodia, East Timor, Laos, Malaysia, Myanmar (formerly Burma), the Philippines, Singapore, Thailand (formerly Siam), Vietnam, and most of Indonesia. For centuries, Southeast Asia has been a center of conflict and upheaval as foreign countries tried to gain control of the region and its rich natural resources. Now, after years of colonial rule by Western powers, the countries of Southeast Asia are independent.

The white elephant has been the symbol of the Thai royal family since the time of King Ramkhamhaeng, who reigned from about 1279 to 1317.

The national flag of Thailand has five horizontal bands. The inner blue band represents the monarchy; the white, purity; and the red, the nation.

Constitution Day in Thailand

Thailand, which has a long history of independence, was the only country in Southeast Asia not colonized by a Western power. For centuries, Thailand was an absolute monarchy, in which the king ruled with supreme authority. Then in 1932, it became a constitutional monarchy, with an elected government. The king, who is still head of state, is highly respected by the Thai people. Constitution Day is celebrated on December 10. Flags and lights decorate offices, shops, and homes. On this day, the Thai people thank the king for allowing them to take part in governing the country.

A huge stone warrior guards the Grand Palace in Bangkok, Thailand. Guardian figures protect royal palaces and Buddhist temples throughout the country.

A statue of Sir Thomas Stamford Raffles, a British merchant who founded modern Singapore in 1819 as a trading settlement, looks over one of the world's busiest cities.

Malaysia and Singapore

On August 31, Merdeka Day (Independence Day), Malaysia celebrates winning independence from Britain in 1957. The road to independence began after World War II. Although the Federation of Malaya was created in 1948, Malaysia remained under British protection for another nine years. With one of the world's busiest ports, Singapore came under British control in 1824 and was occupied by the Japanese from 1942 to 1945. Singapore achieved internal self-government in 1959, joined the newly formed Federation of Malaysia in 1963, and became a fully independent country in 1965.

This is the emblem of the Federation of Malaysia.

SABAH MAJU JAYA

Independence in Indonesia

From 1799 to 1945, Indonesia was a colony of the Netherlands and was known as the Dutch East Indies. During World War II, it was occupied by the Japanese, but in 1945, nationalist leader Sukarno declared Indonesia independent. Sukarno became the nation's first president. The Dutch finally granted Indonesia full independence in 1949. Every year on August 17, Indonesians celebrate Independence Day. Buildings are decorated with lights and flags, and the words *Long live Indonesia*, can be seen everywhere. There are fireworks displays, flag-raising ceremonies, and spectacular parades of floats and marching bands.

A group of dancers in traditional dress marks the 100th anniversary of President Sukarno's birth, on June 6, 2001.

The Commonwealth of the Philippines, a political organization established in 1935, tried to help the Filipinos gain their political and economic freedom. But the Japanese later set up an oppressive government after their invasion during World War II.

Fighting for Freedom

In 1965, military officers tried to overthrow Indonesia's government. Though they failed, Sukarno gradually was forced to give up power to the military leader Suharto, who became president in 1968. In 1976, Suharto's government annexed East Timor (a former Portuguese colony) to Indonesia. Following Suharto's downfall in May 1998, Indonesia was plunged into chaos as various groups and regions began to fight for their own independence. East Timor voted for its independence in a 1999 referendum. It became independent in May 2002 and later changed its name to Timor-Leste.

A poster commemorates Indonesian independence leaders Sukarno, left, and Hatto, right.

Independent Philippines

For almost 400 years, Spain ruled the Philippines. In 1896, an unsuccessful revolt took place against the Spanish. In 1898, control of the islands passed to the United States as a result of the Spanish-American War. On June 12, Filipinos celebrate the country's declaration of independence from Spain in 1898. The Philippines finally gained full independence in 1946.

An Independence Day float passes an enthusiastic crowd in Manila, the capital of the Philippines.

Indian Independence

The flag of modern India consists of an orange stripe representing Hindus, a green stripe representing Muslims, and a white stripe standing for peace. The central wheel is a symbol of Buddhism.

On the stroke of midnight on August 14, 1947, Indian leader Jawaharlal Nehru made a famous speech. "Long years ago," he told those gathered in the Indian Parliament, "we made a tryst with destiny, and now the time comes when we shall redeem our pledge.... At the stroke of the midnight hour, when the world sleeps, India will awake to life and freedom." After centuries of foreign rule and long years of struggle, India became an independent country.

The shield of the British East India Company.

The British in India

During the first half of the 1700's, India's rulers, the Mughals, began to lose power. In their place, the British East India Company expanded its strength and influence. Set up in 1600 to trade with India and East Asia, the company now turned its attention to land and politics. In 1757, it won a battle for the state of Bengal. Over the next 100 years, British territorial control expanded, forming the basis of British rule called the Raj.

The Indian Rebellion broke out in Meerut, near Delhi, and quickly spread. Fighting was fierce and brutal, with high casualties.

Indian soldiers serving in the army of the East India Company were called sepoys.

SOUTH AND CENTRAL ASIA

South and Central Asia are areas of distinct cultures and peoples. These regions form an area at the base of Asia. Asia extends from Africa and Europe in the west to the Pacific Ocean in the east. The northernmost part of the continent is in the Arctic. In the south, Asia ends in the tropics near the equator. South Asia is made up of Afghanistan, Armenia, Bangladesh, Bhutan, India, the Maldives, Nepal, Pakistan, Sri Lanka, the Tibetan plateau in southwest China, and parts of the countries of Azerbaijan and Georgia. Much of India, the largest country in south Asia, forms a peninsula that extends southward into the Indian Ocean. Central Asia includes the countries of Kazakhstan, Kyrgyzstan, Tajikistan, Turkmenistan, Uzbekistan, and the West Siberian Plain.

The Indian Rebellion

In 1857, a widespread rebellion against British rule exploded across northern and central India. This conflict became known as the Indian Rebellion, or Sepoy Rebellion. The trouble was sparked off by the introduction of new practices that offended both Hindu and Muslim soldiers. Many civilians joined in the bloody fighting that followed. With no real leaders, the rebellion was put down by 1859, but both sides harbored anger and bitterness for many years.

South and Central Asia

End of Company Rule

In 1858, the British Parliament took control of the East India Company's Indian possessions. The British government began to govern India directly. A viceroy was appointed to represent the British Crown in India. A secretary of state for India handled Indian matters in London. In 1876, Queen Victoria was officially proclaimed empress of India. British rule in India lasted until India gained its independence in 1947.

Indian National Congress

The Indian National Congress was founded in 1885 as a largely Hindu political party dedicated to pressing the British for a greater share of power for Indians. In 1906, some Muslims formed the separate Muslim League.

Bal G. Tilak *(1856–1920) served as one of the first leaders of the Indian National Congress.*

Queen Victoria *was proclaimed empress of India in 1876, but she never visited India during her long reign (1837-1901).*

Indian leader Mohandas Gandhi *distributes fruits to children in 1944. Considered a saint by many, Gandhi led a spiritual life and gave up all his earthly possessions.*

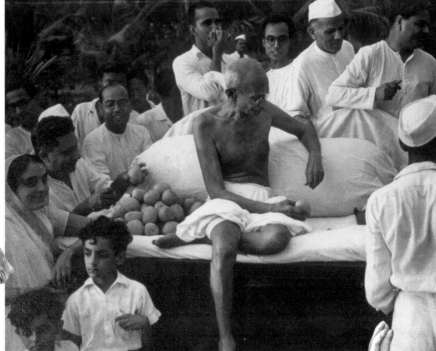

THE FIRST GENERAL ELECTIONS IN INDIA were held in 1951 and 1952.

The Lion Capital is the national emblem of India. *Based on an ancient pillar, the emblem carries the words* Satyameva Jayate, *which mean* Truth Alone Triumphs.

Struggle for Independence

For much of the Raj, Indians had very little say in how their country was governed. Gradually, they began to organize to win back their independence. One of the most important figures in the independence movement was a lawyer named Mohandas K. Gandhi (1869–1948). Known as the Mahatma (Great Soul), he urged Indians to follow his policy of nonviolent struggle against British rule.

Jawaharlal Nehru *(1889-1964), one of the leaders of India's independence movement, became the country's first prime minister.*

Independent India

At first, the Indian National Congress pushed the British to allow Indians greater self-rule. But by the time World War II broke out in 1939, the organization was calling for full independence. The Congress wanted immediate self-government and refused to support the war effort. In 1942, Indian leaders launched a mass civil disobedience movement to force the British to "quit India." Five years later, India became an independent country. The Indian tricolor flag was hoisted on the Red Fort in Delhi, marking the end of British rule.

The Partition of India

In the Pakistani flag, the green color and the star and crescent moon stand for Islam. The white stripe on the left represents the country's other religions and minorities.

The ancient Badshahi mosque in Lahore, Pakistan.

India became an independent country on August 15, 1947, but paid a high price for its freedom. The Muslim League, under the leadership of Muhammad Ali Jinnah, had been campaigning for a separate Muslim state to be carved out of India. The result was a new partition of India, in which the country was divided into mainly Hindu India and mainly Muslim Pakistan. But India could not be neatly divided in two. New boundaries were drawn to create West and East Pakistan. These two areas with Muslim majorities were at opposite ends of the country of India. In the chaos and violence that followed, millions of people were displaced and about a half-million more were killed.

Religious Differences

Religious differences ranked as the main reason for the partition of India. In the aftermath of partition, millions of people fled across the new borders, fearing for their lives if they stayed behind. In the riots that followed, Mohandas Gandhi appealed to Hindus and Muslims alike to live in peace. On January 30, 1948, however, Gandhi was assassinated by a Hindu fanatic who resented his efforts on behalf of Muslims.

IN AN ATTEMPT TO STOP THE RIOTING between Hindus and Muslims in 1948, Gandhi undertook a fast and would not eat or drink until the violence stopped.

Pakistan and Bangladesh

The new country of Pakistan consisted of two parts separated by more than 1,000 miles of Indian territory. In 1971, following a civil war, East Pakistan won independence from West Pakistan and became the independent country of Bangladesh. Since then, Bangladesh has remained one of the world's poorest countries. Pakistan has faced problems of military rule and the growth of Islamic militancy.

In 1988, Benazir Bhutto was elected prime minister of Pakistan, becoming the first female to head an elected government in a Muslim country.

Ongoing Conflict

In recent years, conflicts between religious groups have continued to plague India. In 1992, Hindus and Muslims clashed in Ayodhya, a town in the state of Uttar Pradesh. This followed the destruction of a mosque that the Hindus claimed had been built on the site of an ancient Hindu holy place. In violence that spread to many areas of India, at least 1,200 people were killed.

A Hindu stands at the disputed site of the mosque in Ayodhya.

50 Years of Independence

On August 15, 1997, India celebrated 50 years of independence. In New Delhi, the capital, cheering crowds watched parades and processions. Just before midnight, politicians and other officials gathered to reenact the historic events of the night of August 14, 1947, and to listen to a recording of Nehru's famous speech. In Pakistan, which also marked its 50 birthday in 1997, the prime minister said that the best way to celebrate would be peace between the two countries.

Kashmir Protests

After independence, the Hindu ruler of Kashmir admitted that region to the Indian Union, even though its population was largely Muslim. Since then, India and Pakistan have clashed repeatedly over rival claims to the region. Mounting tensions in summer 2002 brought the two countries to the brink of war. At that time, Pakistan controlled about one-third of Kashmir, while the Indian army occupied the rest.

Kashmiris in Pakistan protest Indian rule in Kashmir on Kashmir Solidarity Day. This day, observed on February 5, is a national holiday in Pakistan.

Children fly Indian flags on Independence Day.

DURING THE 1980'S, SIKHS IN THE PUNJAB began to call for their own independent state, to be called Khalistan. This led to clashes with Indian troops.

During Passover, Jewish people eat a flat cracker called matzo, which is unleavened (has no yeast or rising agent). Eating matzo reminds them of the Jewish flight from Egypt. The Hebrews had baked bread, but they had to flee before it could rise, so they grabbed the unleavened bread and escaped.

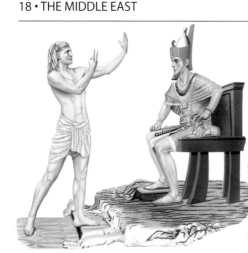

Joseph interprets the pharaoh's dreams.

Passover

Passover, one of the most important Jewish festivals, celebrates the Israelites' escape from slavery in Egypt. Israelites are the ancestors of modern-day Jews. Before Passover, the home is cleaned. All traces of leavened (risen) foods are removed. Devout families use a separate set of cutlery, dishes, and pans during Passover. The seven- or eight-day festival starts with the Seder meal, as Jewish families gather to tell the Passover story from a book called the Haggadah. A plate holds symbolic foods. People eat delicious foods and sing Passover songs into the night. One of the festival's most vital roles is to pass on knowledge of Jewish history to children.

Joseph in Egypt

Joseph was a great-grandson of Abraham, the founder of Judaism. As a teen-ager, Joseph was given a special coat by his father, signifying his future in an important profession. His jealous brothers sold Joseph into slavery. In Egypt, however, Joseph gained a reputation for interpreting dreams. He told the Egyptian pharaoh that there would be seven years of plenty followed by seven years of famine and advised him to store grain for the famine. As a result, the pharaoh put Joseph in charge of the grain storage in Egypt. His prediction came true. He became the second most powerful man in Egypt.

The Egyptian pharaoh Ramses II, who reigned from 1290-1224 B.C., was probably the pharaoh at the time of the Exodus, the escape of the Israelites from Egypt.

The Israelites Enslaved

After the death of Joseph, things grew worse for the Israelites. According to the Bible, the new pharaoh feared that the Israelite population was growing too quickly. He worried that they couldn't be controlled. So the pharaoh decided to make them into slaves. He thought extremely hard labor would make them weaker and they would have fewer children. The Jewish people were forced to work building large palaces and cities.

Baby Moses was hidden in the rushes by the Nile River.

Moses Is Saved

According to the Bible, the pharaoh not only made the Israelites slaves about the late 1300's B.C., but he also ordered that all male Israelite children be killed. One baby boy was hidden in a basket by the Nile River. The pharaoh's daughter found him. She brought him to the pharaoh's palace and named him Moses. The boy was brought up in the palace, with the help of Moses's own mother, as an Egyptian prince.

THE MIDDLE EAST

The Middle East covers parts of northern Africa, southwestern Asia, and southeastern Europe. Scholars disagree on which countries make up the Middle East. But many say the region consists of Bahrain, Cyprus, Egypt, Iran, Iraq, Israel, Jordan, Kuwait, Lebanon, Oman, Qatar, Saudi Arabia, Sudan, Syria, Turkey, United Arab Emirates, and Yemen. The region also is the birthplace of three major religions—Judaism, Christianity, and Islam.

A swarm of locusts destroyed all the remaining plants and crops in Egypt. Earlier, many of the crops had been destroyed by hail.

The Plagues

According to the Torah, God chose Moses to ask the pharaoh to set the Israelites free. The pharaoh refused, and the Egyptians were struck by 10 terrible plagues. The water in the Nile River turned to blood, then frogs covered the land. Lice came, insects swarmed, and all the livestock died. The people were stricken with boils. Hail, locusts, and three days of darkness followed.

Passover

Finally, God warned Moses that in the 10th plague all the first-born sons of Egyptians would die. The Israelites were told to sacrifice a young sheep or goat and smear the animal's blood on the doorpost of their homes. This sign would identify them as Israelites and their sons would be "passed over" and allowed to live. That night, crying was heard all over Egypt as people expressed grief for the loss of their sons. At this point, the pharaoh ordered Moses to take the Israelites out of Egypt.

Moses preaches to the Israelites in a scene on a clay dish. During the long years of wandering in the desert, Moses was an intermediary between God and the Israelites.

An Israelite father smears the blood of a sacrificed sheep or goat on the family's doorpost to identify them as Israelites so God would spare their first-born son at the time of the final plague.

The Exodus

Soon after the Israelites had fled Egypt, the pharaoh and his advisers changed their minds. They missed having the Israelites as slaves to do their work. The pharaoh decided to bring them back and pursued them across the desert with a large army that included hundreds of chariots. As the story goes, just as the Israelites approached the Red Sea, God told Moses to lift his rod and stretch his hand over the waters, which parted. They passed between the two walls of sea. As the Egyptian soldiers arrived, the waves came crashing down again and many Egyptians were drowned. The Israelites were finally free.

A model of an Egyptian infantry company, placed in a tomb to protect the deceased, dates from about 2000 B.C. Egypt had a professional, rigorously trained army of charioteers and infantrymen.

Celebrations of Jewish Identity

This cup is filled with wine for Elijah on Seder night, but it is not drunk. It is believed the Prophet Elijah will one day herald the Messiah.

Throughout the world, Jewish people maintain their faith by praying in synagogues, often using the Hebrew language and continuing the customs and practices of their forefathers. Celebrations and rituals mark the phases of a person's life, including birth, coming of age, marriage, and death. Sacred days and festivals punctuate the religious calendar, including Rosh Ha-Shanah, Yom Kippur, and Passover. In 1948, Jews everywhere celebrated the establishment of the state of Israel.

A man brushes away a piece of hametz with a feather in this illustration from the Middle Ages.

This Seder plate has sections for each of the symbolic foods eaten on Seder night.

Seder Night

On Seder night, Jewish families gather to recount the story of Passover and eat a ceremonial meal. Symbolic foods are placed on the Seder plate. These include bitter herbs in memory of the bitterness of slavery, and Haroseth, made from walnuts, wine, cinnamon, and apples, to represent the mortar the Israelite slaves used when building Egyptian cities. Parsley is dipped into saltwater to remember the slaves' tears.

Removing the Hametz

Just before Passover, Jewish families spring-clean their home. They remove all hametz (leavened foods). One tradition calls for hiding the final bits of hametz around the home. Carrying a candle, the family members hunt for them. As they find each piece, they brush it into a bag with a feather to be burned the next morning. The home is then hametz-free and ready for Passover.

An American rabbi teaches a lesson at a synagogue nursery school.

THE RABBI

The word *rabbi* means my master or my teacher. Rabbis, who are trained in Jewish law, history, and practice, fulfill many roles in the Jewish community. One of their main tasks is to promote Jewish education, and they lead study classes for the community. In synagogue, they lead prayers, read from the Torah, and deliver sermons. Rabbis play an important role in the community, helping the elderly and the sick. The rabbi also talks to people about their problems, advises on spiritual matters, and conducts weddings and funerals. In non-Orthodox traditions, women may become rabbis.

The Founding of Israel

In the late 1800's, a group of Jews started the Zionist movement in response to severe persecution in Europe. They wanted to establish a Jewish homeland in Palestine. Jews began to move there. In 1947, the United Nations agreed to divide Palestine into separate Arab and Jewish states. The Palestinians did not accept this and fighting broke out. The state of Israel was born on May 14, 1948.

Many Jews around the world supported the new Israeli state.

Well-wishers greet the prime minister of Israel *during a visit to the United States.*

Israeli fighter planes flying over the Dome of the Rock in Jerusalem. *Both Palestinians and Israelis want to control the Holy City.*

The Palestinians

Since the founding of Israel, several wars have been fought. Israel gained territory in areas where Palestinian Arabs lived, and many conflicts arose over this situation. After many years of war, the Palestine Liberation Organization signed a peace treaty with Israel, allowing Palestinians to take control of some areas, but the violence and conflict between Israel and the Palestinians still continues.

KNISHES—POTATO PUFFS

- 6 large potatoes
- ½ teaspoon salt
- 6 eggs, lightly beaten
- 6 tablespoons potato starch
- 1–2 tablespoons oil or butter

To make these popular Middle Eastern treats, peel the potatoes and boil them in salted water until tender, about 25 minutes. Drain, then chop in mixer or mash well. Transfer to a large bowl and stir in the beaten eggs. Mix well, then stir in the potato starch. The mixture should be dry enough to shape into balls with your hands. Add more starch if it is still too wet. Place the oil or butter in a baking pan and add the balls of dough. Bake at 350 °F for about 45 minutes, or until the puffs are golden brown.

Guy Fawkes Day

The English Church sails into rough seas *in this illustration.*

James I (1566–1625) had already ruled as James VI of Scotland when he came to the English throne in 1603.

*"Please to remember the fifth of November,
Gunpowder, treason, and plot.
I see no reason why gunpowder treason
Should ever be forgot."*

This old rhyme refers to a famous assassination plot that is commemorated every year in the United Kingdom with bonfires and fireworks. November 5 is called Guy Fawkes Day or Bonfire Night. Although the holiday is based on an infamous act, it celebrates the king of England being saved from disaster. A man named Guy Fawkes plotted with a number of other Catholic conspirators to blow up England's Parliament and king in 1605, but the plot failed.

James I's England

King Henry VIII of England broke away from the Roman Catholic Church because the pope would not annul (cancel) Henry's marriage to his first wife. In 1534, he proclaimed himself supreme head of the Church of England, and 25 years later Elizabeth I made the Church of England a national Protestant institution. Her successor, James I, was a Protestant with a firm belief in the divine right of kings and the absolute power of the monarchy. This stand made him unpopular with Parliament as well as England's Catholics.

Europe and the Americas

The conspirators were led by Robert Catesby, *second from right, who was killed while resisting arrest. Guy Fawkes, third from right, was executed in 1606.*

The Gunpowder Plot

Guido (Guy) Fawkes (1570–1606) and his co-conspirators chose November 5, 1605, the date for the opening of Parliament by the king, for their attack. They rented the house next to Parliament House intending to dig a tunnel between the two buildings, and then place gunpowder into a vault beneath Parliament House. On November 4, Fawkes, who had been chosen to light the powder, went down into the vault to wait until the next day. But a Catholic member of Parliament received an anonymous warning to stay away from the building, the vault was searched, and Fawkes was arrested.

Westminster, London, in the 1800's included, from left to right, Parliament House, Westminster Hall, and Westminster Abbey.

EUROPE

Europe is one of the smallest of the world's seven continents in area but one of the largest in population. Europe extends from the Arctic Ocean in the north to the Mediterranean Sea in the south and from the Atlantic Ocean in the west to the Ural Mountains in the east. The 47 countries of Europe include the world's largest country, Russia, as well as the world's smallest, Vatican City. Russia lies partly in Europe and partly in Asia.

Lighting the Bonfire

On November 5, people in Britain watch fireworks displays and light huge bonfires. Many people make an effigy of Guy Fawkes, called a guy, out of cloth, straw, and other cheap materials. Days before the event, young people display their effigy and ask passers-by for "a penny for the guy." They spend the money they collect on fireworks. When the bonfire is burning well, the guy is thrown on top so that everyone can watch it burn.

The ancient Celtic ritual of building a wicker man is shown in this illustration from the 1800's. When it was finished, the giant effigy was burned to the ground as a form of sacrifice.

Samhain

Bonfire Night also recalls the ancient Celtic celebration of Samhain. This holiday took place at the Celtic New Year in early November, considered a dangerous time when the spirits of the dead walked about. The Celts built large fires, in which they sacrificed produce from their fields. An important Celtic festival, Samhain became associated with the haunted night of Halloween.

Guy Fawkes Day is also known as Bonfire day. Days before the event fire wood is collected for the organized bonfires.

MAKE YOUR OWN GUY

- a pillowcase
- tights
- straw or newspaper
- long socks or sticks
- glue
- buttons
- yarn
- a sewing needle
- a paper cone
- string or rubber bands
- old jacket, pants, hat, gloves (all optional)

Make your own life-sized guy for November 5. Make the body out of an old pillowcase. Make the head from a pair of tights. Stuff it with straw or newspaper and then sew it closed. Pull the legs of the tights through the pillowcase to hold the head on. Stuff long socks and sew them on for arms and legs, or use wooden sticks. Glue two buttons and a piece of yarn onto the head to make eyes and a mouth. Attach a paper cone with string or a rubber band to make the nose. For messy hair, sewn on a bunch of yarn. An old jacket, pants, hat, and gloves can be tied on to dress your guy.

Marie Antoinette (1755–1793), Louis XVI's wife and French queen, was unpopular because of her extravagant lifestyle. A false story was told about her that when she was informed that the people had no bread to eat, she remarked: "Then let them eat cake!" She was guillotined nine months after her husband's execution.

The Bastille held only seven prisoners on the day it was stormed. They were set free, while the prison governor and some of his men were killed. The fortress was later demolished.

Bastille Day

In France, July 14 is Bastille Day. This national holiday commemorates the beginning of the French Revolution in 1789, when the people rose up against their king and demanded greater freedom and more rights. It is a day when all French citizens can celebrate their nation and its history.

Louis XVI (1754–1793) came to the throne in 1774. He showed himself to be a weak ruler who was more interested in personal activities than public affairs.

The Revolution

The storming of the Bastille on July 14, 1789, represented the beginning of the French Revolution. In 1792, the new National Convention proclaimed France a republic, and in January 1793, Louis XVI was led to the guillotine and executed. The French Revolution continued until 1799, when Napoleon Bonaparte seized control of France's government.

The French Monarchy

By the late 1700's, the French nation had been governed by kings for more than 700 years. France had no real parliament and no constitution. The French royal family and nobility lived in luxury, while working people lived in hardship and provided almost all the country's tax revenue.

Storming of the Bastille

The French built the fortress of the Bastille in about 1370 to defend the entrance to Paris. Beginning in the 1600's, the fortress was used as a state prison. It became notorious as a prison for those who dared speak against the king and the state. On July 14, 1789, a huge crowd stormed the Bastille, hoping to find arms and ammunition to defend themselves against the king's army.

Detail of Eugène Delacroix's painting **Liberty Leading the People** *(1830). The red and blue of the tricolor flag represented Paris, and white was the color of the old royal flag.*

Liberty, Equality, Fraternity!

About six weeks after the fall of the Bastille, the National Assembly approved the Declaration of the Rights of Man and of the Citizen. This statement began, "Men are born and remain free and equal in rights," and went on to list these civil rights. It declared that power belonged to the nation, and that authority proceeded from the nation. People were free to express their opinions, and all persons were presumed innocent until proven guilty. "Liberty, equality, fraternity," the revolutionary watchwords, form the French national motto today.

Decorated title of the Declaration of the Rights of Man and of the Citizen.

Troops in the southern French city of Marseilles had their own marching song. When they sang it in Paris in 1792, the Parisians called it "The Marseillaise." The song was adopted as France's national anthem in 1879.

MARCHE DES MARSEILLOIS

A military parade on Bastille Day marches along the Champs Élysées in Paris before the French president, below.

Fireworks *light up the sky behind the Eiffel Tower in Paris.*

Modern Celebrations

French people honor their republic and celebrate their freedom on Bastille Day, which became a permanent national holiday in 1880. The day is filled with parades and speeches. In the evening there are dances, parties, and fireworks displays. People may cry, "Vive le quatorze Juillet!" or "Long live the 14 of July!"

Laurel leaves were an emblem of victory in ancient times. A wreath of laurel leaves forms part of the Greek national emblem.

Greece Expiring on the Ruins of Missolonghi—a detail from the painting by Eugène Delacroix.

Greeks fight under their new flag. The flag was adopted in 1822, during the War of Independence, and readopted in 1978.

Greek Independence

Greek Independence Day on March 25 commemorates the day in 1821 when the Greeks rose up against their Ottoman rulers, who were Muslims. On that day, Bishop Germanos of Patras is said to have raised the Greek flag at his monastery. March 25 is also a very important day in the Christian calendar, celebrating the Annunciation, when the angel Gabriel told the Virgin Mary that she would give birth to Jesus. Greek Orthodox Christians have a double reason to celebrate this holiday with church services, parades, and special ceremonies.

Helping the Greek Cause

Inspired by their studies of ancient Greece, many writers, artists, and scholars became interested in the Greek struggle for independence in the early 1800's. The English poet Lord Byron (1788–1824) set out on a grand tour of Greece and other European countries in 1809. His works and actions inspired others, such as the French artist Eugène Delacroix (1798–1863). The naval fleets of France, Russia, and the United Kingdom all helped the Greeks in their war of independence.

Lord Byron joined Greek fighters in their struggle against the Ottomans. After a sudden illness in Greece, he died.

Defeating the Ottomans

The Ottoman Empire began to take control of Greek lands during the 1300's. A sense of Greek nationalism and cultural revival began growing in the 1700's, culminating in the war that began in 1821. The War of Greek Independence continued until 1829. Otto, a Bavarian prince, became the first head of the newly independent country.

Italian Liberation

On April 25, Liberation Day, Italians celebrate their country's liberation from the Nazis at the end of World War II (1939-1945). By 1945, Italians had spent more than 20 years under the Fascist dictatorship of Benito Mussolini, who was known as Il Duce (The Leader). After his death and the end of the war, Italy became a republic. Liberation Day gives Italians the opportunity to celebrate freedom and honor those who made it possible.

An Italian partisan soldier who fought the Fascists.

Fascism took its name from the fasces, a bundle of rods tied around an axe that was an ancient Roman symbol of power. It appeared with the Italian flag during the Fascist period.

Partisan Resistance

In 1940, the Italian Fascists, led by Benito Mussolini (1883–1945), took Italy into World War II on the side of Nazi Germany. In 1943, members of the government overthrew Mussolini, who became the head of a German-controlled government in northern Italy. After Italy declared war on Germany, civil war broke out between the remaining Fascist forces and a growing movement of anti-Nazi Italians organized by the Committee of National Liberation. In April 1945, underground resistance fighters called partisans killed Mussolini. The following year, the Italians voted to abolish their monarchy and establish a republic.

The Victor Emmanuel Monument stands near the ancient center of Rome.

In Honor of the Past

On Liberation Day, a wreath is placed on the Altar of the Fatherland at the Victor Emmanuel Monument in Rome. This huge white marble monument was dedicated in 1911 in honor of Victor Emmanuel II (1820–1878), the first king of a unified Italy. It also contains a tomb of the Unknown Soldier, who represents those who fought and died for Italy during the two world wars of the 1900's.

Guards place a wreath on the altar of the Victor Emmanuel Monument.

A Soviet passport is jammed onto a railing to show a Lithuanian's rejection of Soviet citizenship.

Emerging Nations

The decline of Communism and the break-up of the Soviet Union (U.S.S.R.) in the 1980's and 1990's led to the creation of many independent states in eastern Europe and central Asia. As oppressive governments were overthrown, people began to express themselves more freely. Ethnic groups used the opportunity to celebrate their individual cultures, including their religious beliefs. In many of the emerging nations, holidays now recognize freedom and individuality.

A statue of a Communist leader is demolished.

Czech dancers whirl in traditional costumes at a folk festival in Straznice.

Independence and Identity

The end of Communism allowed people throughout Eastern Europe to celebrate their independence. Many people felt they had been forced to adopt foreign cultures and traditions, and they were pleased to reassert their own identity. Czechs and Slovaks lived under a Communist regime in Czechoslovakia from 1948 to 1989. After the collapse of the Communist government, the Czech Republic and Slovakia became separate states on January 1, 1993.

A man helps knock down the Berlin Wall, which separated East and West Berlin.

End of the Soviet Union

When Mikhail Gorbachev became Soviet leader in 1985, he launched a series of reforms that eventually led to the collapse of the Soviet Union in 1991. The break-up of the Soviet empire led to the creation of 15 new independent countries. Among them were Russia; the Baltic states of Estonia, Latvia, and Lithuania; the Eastern European states of Belarus, Moldova, and Ukraine; and the central Asian states of Kazakhstan, Turkmenistan, and Uzbekistan.

Knocking Down the Berlin Wall

After World War II, disagreements between the victorious Allies then jointly occupying Germany led to the division of the country into Communist East Germany and non-Communist West Germany. Located in East Germany, the city of Berlin was divided into Communist East Berlin and non-Communist West Berlin. In 1961, the East Germans put up a wall to stop people who were living in East Germany and East Berlin from fleeing to West Berlin. During the late 1980's, mass demonstrations in East Berlin helped bring about the end of the Communist regime in East Germany. In November 1989, the border between East and West Germany was opened, and soon the Berlin Wall came down. Germany was formally reunited on October 3, 1990. That day is celebrated as the Day of German Unity throughout the country.

Political Freedom

Members of a trade union called Solidarity, founded in 1980, fought for political reforms in Poland. In 1989, the Polish government at last agreed to free elections, and Solidarity's candidates were highly successful. In Romania, thousands of people were killed during a popular revolt against the dictatorship of Nicolae Ceausescu. The rebellion succeeded and Ceausescu was overthrown and executed in 1989.

Solidarity leader Lech Walesa won the Nobel Peace Prize in 1983 and became president of Poland seven years later.

Romanians display their national flag from which the Communist symbol has been cut.

Serbs appear in national costumes.

A woman washes clothes in a refugee camp, one of many created by civil wars in the former Yugoslavia.

Ethnic Differences

In the early 1990's, the former Republic of Yugoslavia broke into five nations: Bosnia-Herzegovina, Croatia, Macedonia, Slovenia, and a new Federal Republic of Yugoslavia made up of Serbia and Montenegro. Disputes over borders led to violence and a series of brutal wars between ethnic groups such as Serbs, Croats, and Bosnians.

Freedom of Worship

After the decline of Communism, many communities were able to return to a more traditional way of life. People also gained the freedom to express their faith openly. Many of the former Soviet republics, such as Uzbekistan, have large Muslim majorities. In Kazakhstan, a majority of the people follow Islam, while many others are Orthodox Christians.

Muslims pray at a mosque in Samarqand, Uzbekistan.

American patriot Paul Revere (1734-1818), a silversmith, rode from Boston to Lexington in Massachusetts on the night of April 18th, 1775, to warn the people that British troops were on the move.

PATRICK HENRY (1736–1799), the first governor of the commonwealth of Virginia, made a famous speech against British rule that ended: "Give me liberty, or give me death!"

American Independence

In the United States, Independence Day, held on July 4, commemorates the adoption of the Declaration of Independence on that date in 1776. This document declared that the 13 American Colonies "are, and of right ought to be, free and independent states." At the time, the colonies were at war with Great Britain. By 1783, the Americans had won the war. Six years later, in 1789, the U.S. Constitution went into effect. A revolution that started as a struggle for rights ended with the birth of a nation.

King George III, who reigned from 1760–1820, backed tough British policies that upset the North American colonists.

British Rule

In 1763, Britain began taxing goods imported into the American Colonies, including tea, paper, paint, and glass. As a result, such items became very expensive. American Indian lands west of the colonies were closed to further European settlement, and in 1765 a new Stamp Act required all colonists to pay for stamps on legal documents and newspapers. These measures created a storm of protest in the colonies.

The Boston Tea Party

In 1773, the British Parliament enraged the American colonists by passing a Tea Act, which gave special advantages to the British East India Company. But the colonists retaliated. On the night of December 16, 1773, several British tea-carrying ships were anchored in Boston Harbor. As many as 100 men boarded the ships and dumped their cargo of tea into the water as an act of protest. This event became known as the Boston Tea Party.

Protesters disguised as American Indians dump cases of tea into Boston Harbor.

THE AMERICAS

The continents of North America and South America make up the Western Hemisphere. North America contains Canada, Greenland, the United States, Mexico, Central America, and the Caribbean Sea islands. South America contains Argentina, Bolivia, Brazil (which occupies almost half the continent), Chile, Colombia, Ecuador, Guyana, Paraguay, Peru, Suriname, Uruguay, and Venezuela.

Revolutionary War

The Revolutionary War in America began with a clash between British and American troops at Lexington and Concord, Massachusetts, in 1775. The American minutemen (so called because they were ready to take up arms at a minute's notice) fought the British redcoats, who turned back toward Boston. This battle started a war that lasted until the 1780's. The British lost a decisive battle and surrendered at Yorktown, Virginia, in 1781. The two countries signed a peace treaty in Paris two years later.

British soldiers, called "redcoats" by the Americans, fire on protesters in 1770 in an incident called the "Boston Massacre."

The statue of an American minuteman symbolizes the readiness of these soldiers to fight.

George Washington

George Washington (1732–1799), a leading opponent of British rule, became commander-in-chief of the American forces during the war. He directed troops at the final battle of Yorktown, and in 1789 the Electoral College unanimously chose him to be the first president of the newly formed United States of America. Washington's military and political achievements contributed greatly to making the United States independent.

Washington leads his troops in 1776.

Thomas Jefferson presents the final draft of the Declaration of Independence to John Hancock, seated, *president of the Continental Congress.*

The Declaration of Independence

The draft of the Declaration of Independence, which announced the colonies' independence from Great Britain, was written by Thomas Jefferson (1743–1826). It was adopted on July 4, 1776, and later signed by 56 delegates representing the colonies, including Jefferson, who signed for Virginia. The meeting was held at the Pennsylvania State House, in Philadelphia, which became known as Independence Hall. The original parchment document is displayed in the National Archives Building in Washington, D.C.

An American coin of 1776.

The bald eagle is the national symbol of the United States. It appears on the front of the Great Seal of the United States.

Celebrating Freedom

The Fourth of July, also called Independence Day, is an important national holiday in the United States. Festivities held across the country are intended to be full of fun, but Americans never forget that this is a day for honoring their freedom. It is a time for families to come together out of respect for their country and its independence.

Early Celebrations

The first celebration of American independence took place on July 8, 1776. There was a public reading of the Declaration of Independence in Philadelphia, and the Liberty Bell rang out. The first anniversary of the Declaration was also celebrated with parades and bonfires. By the mid-1800's the tradition had spread across the entire nation.

According to legend, the first Stars and Stripes flag was made by Betsy Ross in Philadelphia in 1776. General George Washington asked her to sew the flag, and she is said to have persuaded him to use five-pointed rather than six-pointed stars.

The famous Liberty Bell broke while ringing after its arrival in the American colonies from England in the 1750's. To mark the U.S. Bicentennial in 1976, the bell was moved near Independence Hall in Philadelphia.

The Statue of Liberty, in New York Harbor, was a gift to the United States from the people of France. Designed to commemorate 100 years of American independence, the statue of Liberty Enlightening the World was made in France, then taken apart and shipped across the Atlantic in packing cases. It was dedicated in 1886.

"The Star-Spangled Banner"

In September 1814, a Baltimore lawyer named Francis Scott Key boarded a British ship anchored off the U.S. coast to arrange the release of an American civilian. On September 13, the British attacked nearby Fort McHenry. When dawn broke the next morning, and Key saw the American flag still flying over the fort, he wrote a patriotic poem, "The Star-Spangled Banner," on the back of an envelope. Key set the words to an existing English tune. The song quickly became popular throughout the United States and was adopted as the official U.S. national anthem in 1931.

Francis Scott Key sees the American flag still flying. "Oh! Say, does that star-spangled banner yet wave," he wrote, "o'er the land of the free and the home of the brave?"

Celebrations Today

In many U.S. communities, the Fourth of July is celebrated with a parade. This usually includes marching bands with lots of drums and baton-twirlers. After the parade, many people have family get-togethers. They often go to a beach, park, or amusement area to play games and enjoy a barbecue or picnic. In the evening, it's time for a fireworks display organized by the local community.

ALL-AMERICAN BARBECUE SAUCE

- 2 tablespoons unsalted butter
- 1 large onion, thinly sliced
- 2 cloves garlic, thinly sliced
- 2 stalks celery, thinly sliced
- 4 tablespoons finely chopped parsley
- 4 tablespoons brown sugar
- 4 tablespoons Worcestershire sauce
- 1 cup ketchup (spicy, if preferred)
- 2 tablespoons white wine vinegar
- $\frac{1}{2}$ cup boiling water

Heat the butter in a heavy-bottomed saucepan over medium heat. Add the onion, garlic, celery, and parsley and sauté for about 5 minutes until transparent. Do not brown. Stir in the brown sugar, Worcestershire sauce, ketchup, vinegar, and water. Reduce heat and simmer for 10 minutes. Slather onto ribs, burgers, or hot dogs, or use for dipping chips or French fries.

Independence Day parades often feature marching bands wearing fancy uniforms and playing patriotic music.

Civil Rights

Juneteenth stands for June 19, the day in 1865 when the slaves of Texas learned that they were free. Since then, African Americans have gained more civil rights, and many welcome the opportunity to celebrate their freedom as a holiday. In January, a U.S. national holiday honors Martin Luther King, Jr., who led the U.S. civil rights movement in the 1950's and 1960's.

The state flag of Texas, called the Lone Star Flag, already existed when Texas joined the Union as the 28th state in 1845, 20 years before the events remembered by Juneteenth.

A gray-clad Confederate fights a flag-bearing Union soldier at Gettysburg, Pennsylvania, in 1863. About 4,000 Confederates and more than 3,000 Union soldiers were killed in this decisive battle.

Abraham Lincoln did not live to enjoy peace after the Civil War. He was assassinated just a few days after the Confederates surrendered in April 1865.

The American Civil War

The Civil War of 1861–1865 was fought between 23 northern (Union) states and 11 southern (Confederate) states. Fearing that President Abraham Lincoln (1809–1865) would abolish slavery in the South, the Confederate states withdrew from the Union. Southern troops fired the first shots of the war at Fort Sumter in South Carolina. When the war ended with Union victory four years later, slavery was officially abolished and slaves gained their freedom.

Uncle Tom's Cabin, by Harriet Beecher Stowe, was published in book form in 1852. It increased Northern anger against the South and caused many people to join the fight for freedom.

135,000 SETS, 270,000 VOLUMES SOLD.

UNCLE TOM'S CABIN

FOR SALE HERE.

AN EDITION FOR THE MILLION. COMPLETE IN I Vol. PRICE 37 1-2 CENTS.
" " IN GERMAN, IN I Vol. PRICE 50 CENTS.
" " IN 2 Vols. CLOTH, 6 PLATES, PRICE $1.50.
SUPERB ILLUSTRATED EDITION. IN I Vol. WITH 153 ENGRAVINGS,
PRICES FROM $2.30 TO $5.00.

The Greatest Book of the Age.

The Emancipation Proclamation

The Civil War resulted in the Union's being saved, and it also ended slavery. On January 1, 1863, Lincoln issued an Emancipation Proclamation, which stated that slaves were free in all areas of the Confederacy that were still in rebellion against the Union. But it was only after the war was over that the proclamation had any effect in Texas. On June 19, 1865, Major General Gordon Granger arrived in the Texas town of Galveston and officially announced that all slaves were free. Later that year, the 13th Amendment to the U.S. Constitution confirmed the abolition of slavery throughout the United States.

Former slaves rejoice at their freedom.

Juneteenth

Juneteenth originated in Texas after the Civil War. Large festivals took place every year in the town of Mexia. Gradually, Juneteenth celebrations spread to other states. In 1980, Texas declared Juneteenth a state holiday. Festivities involve public entertainments, parades, and readings. There are family get-togethers, with barbecues, picnics, and ball games.

Dr. Martin Luther King, Jr., was shot and killed in Memphis, Tennessee, in 1968. A U.S. national holiday honors his birthday on the third Monday in January.

Young tambourine players enjoy their Juneteenth parade.

This boy is leading a group in the annual Martin Luther King, Jr., Day Parade in Miami, Florida.

THE CIVIL RIGHTS MOVEMENT

During the 1950's and 1960's, the U.S. civil rights movement was led by Martin Luther King, Jr., (1929–1968), an African American Baptist minister. In 1956, he successfully campaigned for black people not to have to give up their seats on buses to whites in Montgomery, Alabama, where he and his family lived. In 1963, more than 200,000 people heard King's famous "I have a dream" speech in Washington, D.C., in which he hoped that his children would "not be judged by the color of their skin but by the content of their character." The following year he was awarded the Nobel Peace Prize for leading nonviolent protests against injustice.

Martin Luther King, Jr., Day

On April 4, 1968, Martin Luther King, Jr., was assassinated in Memphis, Tennessee. Many people consider him a hero because of his contribution to the civil rights movement and his policy of nonviolence in the fight for justice and peace. Today Martin Luther King, Jr., is remembered with a national holiday on the third Monday of January each year. The first celebration of Martin Luther King, Jr., Day took place on January 20, 1986. Since then, memorial services and prayer, as well as marches and parades throughout the country, have been part of the special festivities.

Latin American Independence

Most of the countries of Central and South America gained their independence from Spain and Portugal during the first half of the 1800's. Simón Bolívar and other patriots led their people in powerful rebellions against the Europeans. Although the histories of many of the nations are closely bound together, they each celebrate their independence in their own unique way.

This is the Mexican national emblem. According to legend, the ancient Aztecs built their capital where they found an eagle perched on a cactus. This is where Mexico City stands today.

A young Mexican waves his national flag on September 16, Independence Day.

Mexico's Cry for Freedom

On the night of September 15, 1810, a revolutionary priest named Miguel Hidalgo y Costilla called on the people of his town of Dolores to rise up against their Spanish rulers. This began a long struggle for freedom that succeeded 11 years later. Every year on the evening of September 15, the president of Mexico appears on the balcony of the National Palace, rings a historic bell, and recites Hidalgo's famous "Cry of Dolores." The next day, Mexicans celebrate their independence.

Costa Rica

Spanish conquerors arrived in 1502 and named this part of Central America *Costa Rica,* meaning rich coast, because they hoped to find gold there. Although they found no gold, Costa Rica remained a Spanish colony until the 1800's. On September 15, 1821, Costa Rica gained its independence, along with El Salvador, Guatemala, Honduras, and Nicaragua. These countries joined the Mexican Empire, and later formed the United Provinces of Central America. Costa Rica became a separate republic in 1838.

Young Costa Ricans dress in traditional costume for Independence Day, September 15. All over the country there are parades, dances, and fireworks.

Chilean Freedom from Spain

The people of Chile began their revolt against their Spanish rulers in 1810, when a group of landowners formed a ruling council and declared that they would be an independent government. By 1814, however, Spanish forces had regained the country. Then General Bernardo O'Higgins joined with Argentine liberator, José de San Martin, to lead an army across the Andes Mountains from Argentina to Chile. In 1818, they won a final victory over the Spaniards. O'Higgins became the new nation's first leader.

Chileans celebrate their freedom from Spain beneath their new national flag.

The Liberator

Simón Bolívar, one of South America's greatest generals, was known as " The Liberator." This was a good title for the man who helped gain independence for Bolivia, Colombia, Ecuador, Peru, and Venezuela. Yet this was not enough for Bolívar, who created a republic called Gran Colombia from former Spanish possessions. But the republic soon broke up. Bolivia, which was previously Upper Peru, gained independence in 1825 and was named after him.

Simón Bolívar (1783–1830) was born into a wealthy family in the Spanish colony of Venezuela. He traveled to Europe as a young man, and his experiences led him to vow to free his homeland.

Antonio José de Sucre (1795–1830) was the best of Bolívar's generals. His forces defeated the Spainards to win freedom for Bolivia, and he became the newly independent country's first president in 1826.

African slaves harvest coffee in Brazil. A law abolished Brazilian slavery in 1888, just a year before the empire became a republic.

Brazilian Kingdom, Empire, and Republic

In 1815, King John VI of Portugal, who had fled to Brazil, made this colony a kingdom. On September 7, 1822, his son Pedro declared Brazil independent and a few months later was crowned emperor. Pedro's son, Pedro II, took over the empire, and despite a war against Paraguay, Brazil's agriculture and industry prospered. In 1889, Pedro II was forced to resign , and Brazil became a republic. Today, Brazilians still celebrate their independence on September 7.

Pedro I (1798–1834) served as the first emperor of Brazil.

Henri Christophe (1767–1820) fought in the revolution that led to an independent Haiti in 1804. Born a slave, he became president and then king of northern Haiti.

From Colonization to Independence

Many organized states existed in Africa before the European colonial period. In the 1400's, the Portuguese began to explore the west coast of Africa. The European presence grew over the next several centuries until, by the early 1900's, European countries controlled almost all of Africa. It took another 50 years before colonial rule ended in most places.

This portrait of Patrice Lumumba is designed in the shape of Africa. Lumumba became the first prime minister of the independent Congo Republic in 1960. But he was murdered by people wanting control over Congo's mineral wealth.

A French soldier plants the French national flag in the soil of Madagascar, right. Today, it is an independent island country.

TANANARIVE

European Colonization

European nations such as Belgium, Britain, France, Germany, Portugal, and Spain quickly gained more territory in Africa beginning in the mid-1800's. They wanted to control trade farther inland to make more profit from the gold, diamonds, copper, oil, and other natural resources on the continent. European nations also wanted to grow more cash crops, like cotton, which were shipped to factories in Europe and made into goods. In 1884 and 1885, European powers held a conference in the German city of Berlin to decide on how European countries would divide up areas they wanted in Africa.

Antonio Agostinho Neto, right, became president of Angola in 1975. Angola was newly independent from Portugal, but civil war broke out among Angola's three independence movements. After gaining independence, many African states became politically unstable.

A desire for African diamonds led to the British take-over of much of southern Africa.

AFRICA

Africa lies south of Europe and west of Asia and contains 53 independent countries. Tropical rain forests dominate western and central Africa. The world's largest desert, the Sahara, stretches across northern Africa. Africa also has the world's longest river—the Nile. Much of the continent is grassland. In the north, most of the people are Arabs. The great majority of the African population lives south of the Sahara.

Fighting Against Colonialism

Africans fought hard against colonialism. In the 1800's and 1900's, European powers sent armies to put down rebellions. Nigerians, for example, unsuccessfully fought in many areas against British rule until 1919. During the 1930's and 1940's, Africans formed labor and religious groups and other organizations to protest against cruel working practices, poverty, and poor education. They knew that education was the key to fighting for independence. Later, some of the leaders of these organizations helped to form political parties, most of which were banned by the colonial powers. Other leaders created armies that fought against their European rulers. Throughout the 1950's, armed struggles wracked Portuguese-held Angola, British Kenya, French Algeria, and other colonies.

Africa

The Road to Independence

By the end of World War II (1939-1945) only four African nations were independent. These were Liberia in West Africa, Ethiopia in northeastern Africa, Egypt in North Africa, and South Africa. During the 1940's and 1950's, many African leaders from other colonies met to find a way to freedom. Some European leaders, too, realized that it was wrong to stop other peoples from ruling themselves. But there were many problems in colonies where a large number of European settlers held power. By the mid- 1970's, however, most African colonies had gained their independence.

Like these Angolan soldiers in Central Africa, other Africans also formed armies to fight for independence.

Jomo Kenyatta became the first prime minister of Kenya after being imprisoned for challenging colonial rule. Kenya, in East Africa, gained independence in 1963.

These commemorative stamps celebrate the independence of Nigeria, Gambia, and Congo.

After Independence

Since independence, many African countries have been plagued by war, bad leadership, drought, and poverty. But others, like Gabon, in Central Africa, have become stable, democratic countries. Gabon celebrates gaining its independence from France in 1960 with a public holiday and celebrations every year on August 17.

A military band in the Central African nation of Gabon leads an Independence Day celebration.

Freedom in South Africa

South Africa was an unusual colony. Dutch settlers, known as Boers, had farmed inland areas of South Africa since the 1600's. The British gained control of the region in the early 1800's. The Boers and the British fought over South Africa in the Anglo-Boer War of 1899-1902. In 1910, the Union of South Africa was formed within the British Empire, with the whites having almost complete power. South Africa's nonwhite majority population was treated appallingly throughout most of the 1900's. They finally gained participation in the government in 1994.

Daniel F. Malan was the leader of the National Party that introduced apartheid laws in South Africa in 1948.

Signs like this were posted in public places where only whites were allowed to go. The sign is written in Afrikaans as well as English.

Living Under Apartheid

Apartheid is an Afrikaans word meaning separateness. In South Africa, it was also the name of a legal system that divided whites and nonwhites in every aspect of their lives. The system was introduced in South Africa in1948 by the ruling white National Party, which wanted to keep the government white. The laws separated people of different races and gave white people better opportunities than nonwhites.

Under apartheid, even bridges were divided into black and white halves. So, too, were buses and trains. "White" beaches were closed to black people.

Archbishop Tutu Works for Peace and Justice

Desmond Tutu became an archbishop in the Anglican Church in South Africa. But his life, too, was affected deeply by the laws of apartheid. As a priest, he was given the chance to travel to other countries. There, he was amazed to see blacks and whites living side by side. When Desmond Tutu returned to South Africa, he encouraged nonwhites to take part in peaceful protest. He publicly urged other nations to stop trading with South Africa until all its people had equal rights. He and Nelson Mandela won the Nobel Peace Prize in 1993.

Archbishop Desmond Tutu led South Africa's Truth and Reconciliation Commission, which worked to heal the scars of apartheid.

The Struggle Against White Rule

Nonwhites fought hard against the South African government. They opposed laws that required blacks to carry passes, which restricted their free movement around the country. They joined organizations to fight for change. But in 1960, the government banned the African National Congress (ANC) and other antiapartheid movements. So the organizations began to fight South Africa from neighboring countries. White rule and the apartheid system were criticized both from inside and outside South Africa. Violent disturbances in Soweto and elsewhere in the late 1970's led to the deaths of many blacks. Many countries reduced their economic ties with South Africa. Gradually, apartheid laws were repealed. In 1990, President F. W. de Klerk lifted the bans on the ANC and other black organizations.

Members of the African National Congress demonstrate against apartheid. They also demand the release of Nelson Mandela.

Black and white voters stood in line together in 1994, sometimes for many hours, to vote in South Africa's first elections open to all races.

After his release in 1990, Nelson Mandela helped the South African government dismantle apartheid and plan free elections for all. In 1993, he and then-President F. W. de Klerk of South Africa won the Nobel Peace Prize.

Mandela's Freedom

Nelson Mandela, the son of an African chief, studied hard and became a lawyer, using his skills to fight apartheid. In 1962, he was accused of trying to overthrow the government. At his trial, he said: "I have carried the ideal of a democratic and free society in which all persons live together in harmony. It is an ideal for which I am prepared to die." Imprisoned for 27 years, he became a symbol of resistance. So when President F. W. de Klerk legalized the ANC in February 1990, he also released Mandela from prison. After the elections, Nelson Mandela became president in May 1994.

This Inkatha shield belongs to a soldier of South Africa's Zulu people. In 1975, Mangosuthu Buthelezi revived the Inkatha Freedom Party (IFP), which had been founded in the 1920's, to support the Zulu monarchy. The IFP has supported the formation of an independent Zulu state.

Freedom!

Freedom Day on April 27 commemorates South Africa's first democratic elections, held in 1994. It celebrates the end of apartheid and the beginning of democracy. Concerts, arts performances, and parades take place. Freedom Day is also a day to remember all the people who were imprisoned or lost their lives in the fight for justice. Inequality still exists in South Africa. Most nonwhites are still very poor. But many communities are joining together to build their own homes and schools—their own future.

A traditional Maori hei-tiki pendant is made of greenstone.

Australasia and Oceania

Australia and New Zealand

National holidays of Australia and New Zealand commemorate European colonization in the 1700's and 1800's. New Zealand's Waitangi Day celebrates a treaty presented by the British government to the native Maori people. Although people disagree over the treaty's meaning and scope, the holiday offers all New Zealanders an opportunity to celebrate their nation. Australia Day commemorates the founding of that country's first European colony. In recent years, efforts have been made to include Aborigines in the celebrations.

A Maori chief signs the treaty at Waitangi, in the Bay of Islands, on February 6, 1840. Captain William Hobson represented the British government.

A Maori displays traditional face tattoos.

The Treaty of Waitangi

European settlers first arrived in New Zealand in the 1700's. The Maori people had lived on that land for many hundreds of years. The newcomers introduced firearms, increasing warfare between Maori tribes. In 1840, some Maori chiefs signed the Treaty of Waitangi, which promised them British protection and gave them rights to their lands, stipulating that any sales should be only to the British government. Because Maori land was held communally rather than by individuals, some chiefs refused to sign the treaty.

AUSTRALASIA AND OCEANIA

Australasia and Oceania lie east of Asia and west of the Americas. Australasia refers to Australia, New Guinea, New Zealand, and other nearby islands. New Guinea and New Zealand are also considered as part of the Pacific Islands, or Oceania. Oceania is a name given to a group of many thousands of islands scattered across the Pacific Ocean. New Guinea is the largest island in the group. It contains Irian Jaya, which is a part of Indonesia, and the independent country of Papua New Guinea. Islands near the mainland of Asia (Indonesia, Japan, the Philippines) are part of Asia. Islands near North and South America (the Aleutians, the Galapagos) are grouped with those continents. Australia is itself a continent.

Maori Tribes

The Maori people are Polynesians who sailed from islands located northeast of New Zealand about A.D. 1000, or earlier. Legend says that the first Maoris arrived in seven canoes. Today, they speak English, though some also speak the Maori language. Maoris make up about 15 percent of New Zealand's population. The remainder consists of people of European descent, mainly British, known as pakehas, which is Maori for white people. Waitangi Day, on February 6, commemorates the signing of the Treaty of Waitangi and the country's nationhood. In 1974, the name Waitangi Day was changed to New Zealand Day, but the name was changed back again two years later.

Maori singers perform in traditional dress.

PAVLOVA

- 6 egg whites
- 1 ½ cups granulated sugar
- 1 ½ tablespoons corn starch
- 1 ½ teaspoons white vinegar
- 1 cup sliced strawberries
- 2 medium kiwi fruit, sliced
- 1 cup whipped cream

Preheat the oven to 250 °F. Cover a baking sheet with waxed paper. Beat the egg whites in a large bowl with an electric mixer on high speed until soft peaks form. Gradually add the sugar, beating until it is dissolved between each addition. This will take about 10 minutes. Carefully fold in sifted corn starch and the vinegar. Reserve one-third of the meringue mixture and spoon the rest into a circle about 8 to 9 inches across on the baking sheet. Drop spoonfuls of the reserved meringue evenly around the edge of the circle. Bake the meringue circles for about 11/2 hours, or until dry and crisp to touch. Turn the oven off and, with the oven door ajar, leave the pavlova to cool inside. Cover with strawberries and kiwi. Decorate with additional kiwi and whipped cream before serving.

Rosemary, and laurel are symbols of remembrance on Anzac Day.

The Roll of Honour Wall at the Australian War Memorial displays the names of the men and women who lost their lives in battle. On Anzac Day, red poppy flowers are placed next to many of the thousands of names remembered there.

Captain Arthur Phillip (1738–1814) was the founder and first governor of New South Wales.

Australia Day

Australia Day, held on January 26, commemorates the day in 1788 when a convoy of ships called the First Fleet arrived at Sydney Cove. Captain Arthur Phillip had sailed from England with 11 ships carrying British seamen, marines, and officials, and hundreds of male and female convicts. The settlement he founded grew into the city of Sydney. The day was first celebrated as a public holiday in 1833, though the name Australia Day was not introduced until 1931.

Remembering the Anzacs

The Anzacs were soldiers in the Australian and New Zealand Army Corps who served in Europe and the Middle East during World War I (1914–1918). On April 25, 1915, Anzac forces landed at Gallipoli, in Turkey. The campaign against the Turks lasted for eight months and by the end, more than 10,000 Anzacs had been killed. Since the 1920's, Anzac Day has been a public holiday in Australia and New Zealand. Today, Anzac Day commemorates all those who died in war.

Glossary

Abolish To destroy or get rid of something.

Altar A table or raised platform on which offerings are placed, usually found in churches or temples.

Ancestral Something belonging to a family member from a preceding generation to whom you are directly related, for example a grandfather or great-grandfather.

Annex To take over an area or territory and make it a part of a larger country or state.

Anthem A song or hymn sung in praise or loyalty to a leader or country.

Assassinate To kill a leader or political figure.

Asylum A place of safety and protection away from one's homeland.

Brutal Extremely cruel or severe, causing pain and suffering.

Campaign A planned operation to achieve a certain goal or end.

Cash crop A crop, such as cotton or tobacco, which is grown primarily for market sale.

Colony A settlement established by people outside their native land and ruled by the mother country.

Commemorative An event or object that remembers a special historical or religious occasion.

Communism A political, social, and economic system in which most or all property is owned by the state and is supposed to be shared by all.

Conflict A fight or struggle between two or more opposing nations or groups.

Congregation A gathering or assembly of people, usually meeting to worship God or receive religious instruction.

Conquest The act of acquiring something, such as land or territory, by force.

Constitution A document containing the basic laws and principles of a state or nation, and determining the power and rules of a government.

Convict A person found guilty of a crime and serving a prison sentence as punishment.

Delegate A person acting as a representative for a country or state at a conference or convention.

Descendant A blood relative of a previous generation. A child is a descendant of his or her parents, grandparents, great-grandparents, and so on.

Dictatorship The term of office or control of a ruler with absolute power and leadership.

Effigy A stuffed figure, which is beaten or burned, that is made to represent a disliked person.

Exile The state of having been forced to leave one's native country.

Famine Shortage of food for a long period of time.

Fascism Any system of government in which property is privately owned, but all industry and labor are regulated by a strong national government, while all opposition is rigorously suppressed.

Freedom fighter A person who is involved in armed fighting against an unfair government.

Fundamentalism A strict religious movement opposed to change based on rigid and traditional principles.

Grief Emotional distress and suffering, especially felt after the death of someone close.

Heritage Tradition, cultural identity, or property passed down from earlier generations.

Indigenous people Natives, original people living in a country or area before other people settled there, and their descendants.

Infantry Foot soldiers who form part of a larger army.

Isolated Being or feeling alone or separated from others.

Labor group A recognized group of workers who are united in their struggle for better working conditions.

Messiah Any person claimed or thought to be a savior, liberator, or deliverer.

Monarchy A territory or country ruled by a king or queen.

Monastery A place where a community of religious people, such as monks, live.

Mutiny Rebellion against and refusal to obey authority.

Oppression The act of exercising cruel and excessive power and authority over people or a nation.

Oust To remove a person or government forcefully from office and take away their power and authority.

Partition The action of dividing a country into separate states or nations.

Patriotic Great love or devotion for one's country.

Persecution The punishment or harassment of a person or group of people. People might be persecuted because of religion, race, or gender.

Plague A fatal disease that spreads easily and kills many people.

Plot To plan a secret course of action or scheme.

Protest To make a strong objection against something.

Referendum The act of submitting a matter to a direct vote.

Refugee A person who has left his or her community or country to escape danger.

Regime A form of government or administration in which one group of people has total power.

Sacrifice The killing of an animal, which is offered to a god or gods as part of worship.

Slavery The condition of being being forced to work without pay. A slave is someone who is the property of another person, and has no personal rights or freedom.

Somber Having a serious nature.

Stipulate To express a particular condition or promise within an agreement.

Treaty A written contract or agreement between two political authorities.

United Nations (UN) An organization of nations that works for world peace and security and the betterment of humanity.

Upheaval A period of great social disorder and disruption that is often violent in nature.

Urge To encourage or press someone to do something in a forceful and persistent manner.

Viceroy A person who governs a state or country and acts as the representative of the ruling king or queen.

Withdrawal The removal or retirement of a person or body into a less prominent position.

Index

With thanks to Selina Hastings, who made the initial selection of rhymes.

Introduction by David Lloyd.

Illustrations copyright © 1985 by Charlotte Voake

Published in the United States of America by Clarkson N. Potter,
Inc., One Park Avenue, New York, New York 10016.

Originally published in Great Britain by Walker Books Ltd.,
184-192 Drummond Street, London NW1 3HP.

CLARKSON N. POTTER. POTTER and colophon are trademarks of
Clarkson N. Potter, Inc.

Manufactured in Italy

Library of Congress Cataloging in Publication Data
Main entry under title:
Over the moon, a book of nursery rhymes.
    Includes index.
        Summary: An illustrated collection of
traditional nursery rhymes.
    1. Nursery rhymes. [1. Nursery rhymes]
I. Voake, Charlotte, ill.
PZ8.3.O94   1985   398'.8   85-6410
ISBN 0-517-55873-4

10 9 8 7 6 5 4 3 2 1

First American Edition 1985